Mad Honey Symposium

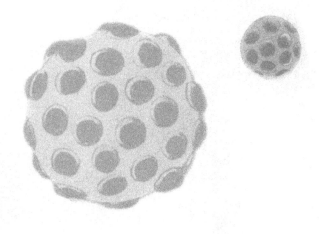

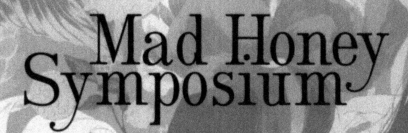

Mad Honey Symposium

SALLY WEN MAO

ALICE JAMES BOOKS

FARMINGTON, MAINE

10 9 8 7 6 5 4 3 2 1

Alice James Books are published by Alice James Poetry Cooperative, Inc.,
an affiliate of the University of Maine at Farmington.

Alice James Books
114 Prescott Street.
Farmington, ME 04938
www.alicejamesbooks.org

Library of Congress Cataloging-in-Publication Data

Mao, Sally Wen
  [Poems. Selections]
  Mad honey symposium / Sally Wen Mao.
     pages cm
  ISBN 978-1-938584-06-0 (pbk.)
  I. Title.
  PS3613.A623A6 2014
  811'.6--dc23
                              2013040198

Alice James Books gratefully acknowledges support from individual donors, private
foundations, the University of Maine at Farmington, and the National Endowment for
the Arts.

ART WORKS.
arts.gov

Cover art: "Secret Jungle" by Angie Wang

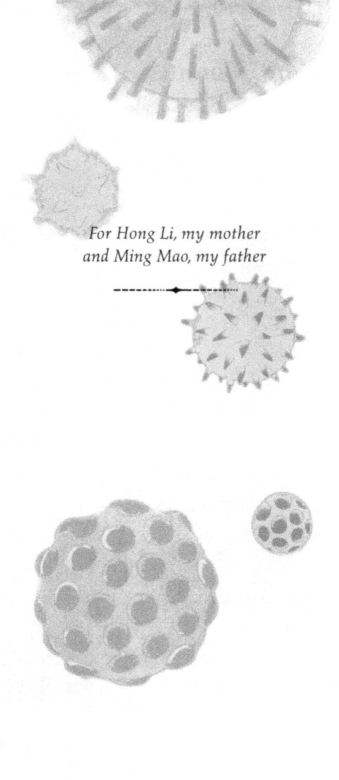

*For Hong Li, my mother
and Ming Mao, my father*

Table of Contents

I.

1	Valentine for a Flytrap
2	Apiology, with Stigma
5	XX
7	*Mellivora Capensis*
10	Mad Honey Soliloquies 1-3
13	On the Sorrow of Apiary Thieves
15	Sonnets for Kudryavka
18	Flight Perils
21	The White-haired Girl
23	The Pickpocket

II.

33	Searching for the Queen Bee
35	Hurling a Durian
37	*Monstera Deliciosa*
38	The Azalea Eaters
41	Capsaicin Eclogue
42	Mad Honey Soliloquies 4-6
47	The Spring of Terrible Fevers
50	The Bullies
51	Lessons on Lessening
53	Song, with Caution Tape
55	Suspension Theory
61	Honey Badger Palinode

III.

65	Migration Suite

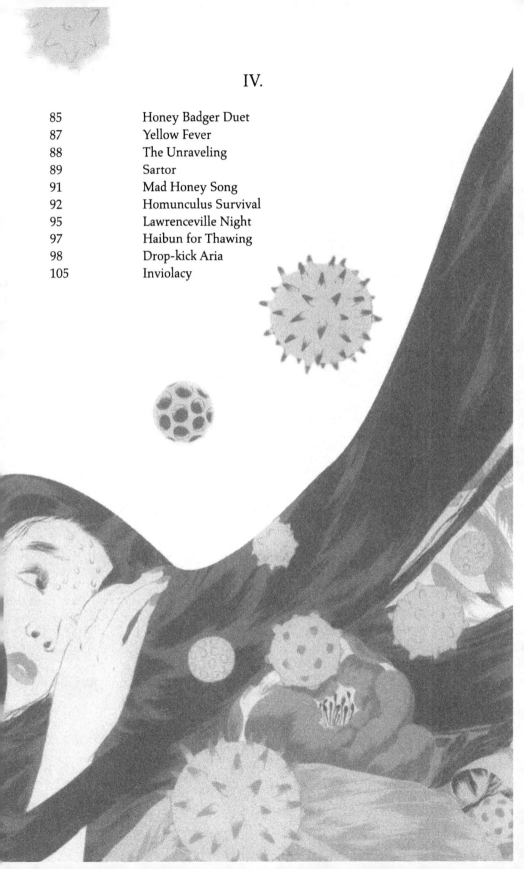

IV.

85	Honey Badger Duet
87	Yellow Fever
88	The Unraveling
89	Sartor
91	Mad Honey Song
92	Homunculus Survival
95	Lawrenceville Night
97	Haibun for Thawing
98	Drop-kick Aria
105	Inviolacy

Acknowledgments

Many thanks to the editors of the following journals, who published these poems in their first forms:

Another Chicago Magazine: "Mellivora Capensis"
Beloit Poetry Journal: "Mad Honey Soliloquies 4-5" and "Migration Suite" section 4
Cave Wall: "Valentine for a Flytrap," "Lawrenceville Night"
The Cincinnati Review: "Honey Badger Palinode"
Colorado Review: "Capsaicin Eclogue"
Cream City Review: "Monstera Deliciosa"
CutBank: "Hurling a Durian," "The Azalea Eaters"
DIAGRAM: "Sartor"
diode: "Lessons on Lessening"
Drunken Boat: "The Bullies"
Guernica: "Honey Badger Duet"
Gulf Coast: "XX"
Hayden's Ferry Review: "Yellow Fever"
Indiana Review: "The White-haired Girl"
The Journal: "Haibun for Thawing"
The Margins: "Apiology, with Stigma," "Mad Honey Soliloquies 1-3" and "Mad Honey Soliloquies 6," "Migration Suite" sections 1-3 and 5-10, and "Drop-kick Aria"
Memorious: "Homunculus Survival"
New Madrid: "Song, with Caution Tape"
Passages North: "On the Sorrow of Apiary Thieves"
Post Road Magazine: "Flight Perils," "Sonnets for Kudryavka"
Quarterly West: "The Unraveling," "Searching for the Queen Bee"
RHINO: "Inviolacy," "The Spring of Terrible Fevers"
Sycamore Review: "Suspension Theory"
"XX" is anthologized in *The Best American Poetry 2013*, selected by Denise Duhamel.

I am indebted to many communities, teachers, mentors, peers, and other fellow artists who have conversed, conspired, and celebrated with me through this journey. To my invaluable mentors at Carnegie Mellon and Cornell, who have guided me through the development of this manuscript from scraps to fruition: thank you, truly. Thank you, Terrance Hayes, Kenneth McClane, Alice Fulton, Yona Harvey, Lyrae Van Clief-Stefanon, Jane McCafferty, and Jim Daniels. Thank you to Dave Eggers and Vendela Vida at 826 Valencia, and to G.C. Waldrep and K.A. Hays at the Bucknell Seminar for Younger Poets.

Thank you to my wonderfully nurturing community of poets fiercer and yet more vulnerable than any honey badger, Kundiman. My gratitude goes to Jennifer Chang, Joseph Legaspi, Soham Patel, Oliver de la Paz, Vikas Menon, Cathy Linh Che, R.A. Villanueva, Sarah Gambito, and so many other incredible fellows and mentors I've had the privilege to meet and befriend for life. To Alice James Books, especially Tamiko and Carey, thank you for giving me this vital platform. Finally, love and gratitude to my friends (you know who you are, you lovely freaks!), and my family. Thank you for giving me courage, strength, and wonder despite short days, cold breath, and the sun disappearing behind the trees.

I.

Valentine for a Flytrap

You are a hairy painting. I belong to your jaw.
Nothing slakes you—no fruit fly, no cricket,
not even tarantula. You are the caryatid
I want to duel, dew-wet, in tongues. Luxurious
spider bed, blooming from the ossuaries
of peat moss, I love how you swindle
the moths! This is why you were named
for a goddess: not Botticelli's *Venus*—
not any soft waif in the Uffizi. There's voltage
in your flowers—mulch skeins, armory
for cunning loves. Your mouth pins every sticky
body, swallowing iridescence, digesting
light. Venus, let me swim in your solarium.
Venus, take me in your summer gown.

Apiology, with Stigma

*Stigma, n. (in flowers) the female part of the pistil
that receives pollen during pollination*

For Melissa W.

There is no real love in the apiary.
Hive mentality: 1. Fatten until you reign

your country on a throne of propolis.
2. Copulate until you explode

with larval broods. Honey makes me sick,
and so does the Queen Bee. Even

in sleep, I see the arrows point at drones
stuck to the ceiling, sparkling spastically

like the sequins on a girl's yellow prom
dress. Some girls pray to be Queen.

They think: wouldn't it be terrific, to be
wanted like that. Wouldn't it be terrific,

to be stroked and adored, to lose your virginity
in the glorious aftermath of royal jelly.

Wouldn't it be terrific to roost, rest, be the envy
and the mother of all. But one girl turns

the other way. At lunch she eats green tea mochi
on the edge of the field, scouts unpopulated

places—a lemon tree, a barberry bush.
Dreading assemblies and cafeterias, she ducks

under the library's front steps, smuggling
field guides or *National Geographics*

with covers of jewel beetles and capybaras,
counting the minutes until recess is over

and biology begins. The price of sincerity:
when the honeybee shucks the anthers

from the camellia, an anthem begins.
It's a slow soprano. An anathema. It screams

from deep inside its ribs. It's a blues,
an aria, an index of heartbreaks. It may break

a thousand mirrors before the pollen descends,
ashes over caldera. Split gorge. Fever. Finally,

the bee pollinates the stigma. The girl curse
sounds like that—a drone of flaws announcing

each maladaptive limb, freckle, admittance
of shame. How to battle this monster?

It is known that Japanese honeybees grew
immune to the vicious Asian giant hornet

by laying a trap: 1. Lure him into the threshold
of an open hive. 2. Besiege him—surround

the saboteur with a wall of impenetrable
bodies. 3. Vibrate until the temperature

reaches 115°F. 4. He will die from the heat
and carbon dioxide. His husk will break,

his heft will plummet. I don't teach my girls
to brave the violence of sun, sons, or stings.

When resources run out, don't sit there and behave.
Abandon hive. If the hornet breaks the heat net,

save yourself. Abandon yen. Abandon majesty.
Spit the light out because it sears you so.

XX

The night my sex returned, I shut the door,

barricaded it with a rattan chair. The banging

curdled the egg pudding and for ten minutes

it was all tremor, all the time. There my mother

was, half-asleep in her gender, and there my sister

was, locked inside her purity panoply. And I, shut

inside, obsessed with the insides of me, obsessed

with the open-and-close of me, dead-sexed, hyper-

sexed—I couldn't stop mulling over how every seed

burst, pummeled into pulp, jejune nectarine jabbed

to the pit. Could anyone forget—the horrible panache

of fruit? I despised softness, how a bite can sluice

flesh. I wanted to disperse like creosote

in water; I wanted to reproduce like spores, tease

like those stars seen so plainly out in the thawing sky

but nonexistent, having exploded long ago.

So entered sex, who loaded a carcass, asphyxiated

creature, into the open suitcase. We shut it tight,

zipped it, but the miasma stayed with us, angry visitor,

as breath on the cinders, as grease in my hair.

Mellivora Capensis

The honey badger (Mellivora capensis) *holds a reputation as the world's most fearless creature (Guinness World Records, 2002) for catching rattlesnakes, invading beehives, hunting porcupines, and fighting larger predators.*

Honey-eater of the cape—body skunk-like, maw
of bones & soil: here is the honeycomb

where your heart surrenders. Here is the snake hole
where your body lies waiting. Under the acacia

you caper, you dance. Under the hives you shiver,
you prowl; oh puff adder, ibex, blood hook

& bees: what can the sand or teeth believe?

The sun rises over
Elephant grasses.

We are everywhere

Assassinating wind.
For prey,

We pray. Bee-trill

Humming viciously

Against chest drum.
Snakes splinter

As gutted shrapnel.

                              Our parched mouths. Birds
                              Flap wildly.

Open my jaw: raw
The meat I swallow,

                              Tender the mouths I bury.

Everywhere this viscous

                              Rapture of stings.

---------•---------

A broken badger is not a sad thing.
When the porcupine quills pierce her gullet
            she does not wince.
When she wanders through the fire factory
            she does not flinch.
When the leopard eviscerates the antelope
            she does not malinger.
When the shower of bullets rips through the woods
            she does not hide.
When the snake whispers venom into her throat,
            she does not whimper.
A broken badger is not a sad thing.

---------•---------

Spit me out, larger beast—find my paws
on your jaw, on your hipbone, on your feet.
Find my breath in your beehive.
Find my mouth on your pendulum.
Find your pendulum knotted, gutted.

Out of its socket like a blood-dipped
locket. Find the waterbuck heaving
in the swamp. Find gashes. Find heat.
Find skin molting but you won't find me.

Mad Honey Soliloquies

Case Study: Kayseri, Turkey, September 2008

1.   [Patient: Husband]

My wife spread-eagles in a quiet room.
One teaspoon each morning of red
honey, incarnadine gamble.

A bid to bury our compulsions—
for our bed to open up and swallow us, hard
into its gullet. Each night one head

stampedes the other, twin eagles shot
in this province. The missives,
misgivings, spill our sheets afoul.

Is this pulse worth saving
in 2008? Friends cautioned
against the honey. Histories chimed in:

entire armies murdered. Remember Pompey?
Remember Xenophon? How the warnings purr
gently on that bed. Instead, it grows moist

with hives, spears of laurel. Yellow splendor
pumping water into the mouths that need it.
The promise of voltage, always enough.

2.   [Patient: Wife]

We were certain it would lift
us from our sagging sheets.

After enough teaspoons, that first
week we finally reached

for each other's bodies. Did I expect
electricity? A charge to elucidate

the fitful nerves on our fingers?
My seams, all splitting?

Something about the sealed
jar, the black market. He spoon-fed

me the sweetness. It felt ecstatic.
Like I was infant, sucking

up sticky milk. Sick, as if we were wrecking
some sanctified memory.

We guzzled tea afterward
and its bitter burn scraped

our insides. Ancient pain—
the ruin of votive gods rusting.

Emergency: blades began spading
our chests. Our hearts split, shut

down. When the ambulance
came, my husband was already another

color. His tongue slipped out.
In its shade I saw a golden dart frog.

3.   [Cardiologist]

That morning, a middle-aged couple checked in for chest
pain, dazed as schoolchildren. What we found: bradycardia.
Their heart rates, nadirs at 35, 45 beats per minute.
Between tests, they mouthed the word *honey,* and the nurses

thought that it was romance—that this pitiable union
of arrhythmias could brace their connubial nest.
But then we found traces of mad honey they'd ingested
to revive desire, as if poison answered all the questions

about their bodies. In my life, many patients
have asked about the heart. How to hush its palpitations.
I have no easy answer for why the wishes that charge
angina pectoris endanger it, put it to sleep.

On the Sorrow of Apiary Thieves

Beekeepers warn: *the good honey's gone.*
All of it's been harvested. What's left
    is chaff, summer's dead

matter. Give up, intruders: this season,
the bees won't wake, and the honey
    of their sleep is noxious.

It is said that when bees can't migrate,
they hibernate in a dragnet of bodies
    around the queen, rotating outward

for warmth so no one dies. But somewhere
in the outskirts, a worker bee might fall
    into a coma, envision a lighthouse

of nectar, daisy stamens trapped in royal
jelly. She must've dreamt this, drifting farther
    from the nucleus of spit-warmth

and swaying. There is no place for dreamers
like her in a complex system: metropole
    of honeyless apiary, its deadbeat

machinery. I can't explain my trespassing
with something simple, like the yen for honey,
    or humectants for a lady's quondam

queendom. The hive breathes all the wishes
I don't have. Empty haven, lantern of viands—
    I almost miss the way the searchlights

once chased me past the topiaries—
footprints striating the damp loam
    along the knoll, toward the bees:

what quiet, what hum. This time, I take only
the frozen ones, those harmless luminaries
    whose heat mends the snow.

Sonnets for Kudryavka

KUDRYAVKA, BEFORE SPUTNIK

Toast to you, dog, for your solar-powered
organs. Your smelt muscles sing. The slag
on your bones cannot die on this earth.
From dumpster to rocket ship, the true
rags-to-riches tale—and it's not even
happening to a human. Not even happening
in America. World-famous gutter-sucker,
tonight you give birth to a new name: Laika.
Before any dog impregnates you, you will shoot
off into the galaxy. Mammal as asteroid,
ultimate runaway. Who are you, whose kismet
matches the greats—a martyr for thought,
like Socrates? Will you drink the hemlock
of space? You, Laika, original cosmonaut?

KUDRYAVKA'S SOBRIQUETS

Zhuchka, little bug: stray mutt covered
in snow—how many tulips have you eaten
since spring? How many cabbages drenched
in ruined milk? *Limonchik,* little lemon:
as a stray, you knew hunger so well you wrecked
your own mouth. In Moscow, they squeezed
lemons over your coat. The seeds stuck
to your damp fur, but the juice disinfected
you. As you licked your own neck, the taste sang

through your tongue. You howled and howled
and it opened your flesh and you were made
invincible. *Laika,* barker: you are that dog
whose face shined in red paint. You are that dog
they renamed so they can silence you again.

KUDRYAVKA IN THE CAPSULE

If your fate were fairer, you'd have traveled
the world on tour. Tongue wagging out,
you'd have felt the siroccos squirming
over your fur, the waters of clear brooks
softening it. You'd have tasted the meats
of animals you could never outrun. You'd
have chased them anyway, across mesas,
icescapes—the reindeer, you'd have gnawed
their fuzzy antlers. Gentle admirers would
pet you, take you in their arms. But now,
nothing sheathes your spinning aorta.
The clock runs faster than your legs
at their hungriest. You are strapped to drill
into oblivion, impale it like a breathing rapier.

KUDRYAVKA: LIFTOFF

Shuttered in hot light and oil-seared stars,
you alone carry the weight of planetary
anxieties. The heat rises and your skeleton
quivers. A vatic singsong proclaims onslaught.
You panic but eat. It is a sticky gel and not
the mutton you were fed yesterday.

But yesterday is extinguished, and even
today and tomorrow have kidded you,
escaped. You are alone with your breathing.
Your lungs plump. You cannot understand
the machine of your solitude, its axles,
its weights. Outside, there is the timber
galaxy. You wake to terror and lumber fast
into the death that's at least known.

Flight Perils

I.   [Love the flightless, learn the dirt, live to stomp]

Once I read the story of a girl
who loved a flightless creature.

> *Leda, hurry and run,*
> *for your swan is waking.*

In the cool willow, his fitful
grip surprised her. Her story bled
into its cloth. All the secrets in the dirt
reneged and built a bridge between enemies.

> *What you need now is more than love.*

At times I tromp the earth
searching for precision. As the sediment
flies away, I trust that worms still live here.
The suicidal swan walks into the tracks.

II.   [Night swallowed all the juncos on Beacon Street]

The second death in my childhood
was a crested eagle, snagged
in cannon-netting as it left its aerie
                for the first time.

I lived on this street. Overhead, a dozen juncos

saw-toothed over marquisette.
3/4ths of a flock struck
in an electrical storm.

When I picked one up, its plume
                    showed no sign of lightning,
                    though its humerus bone

shattered to bits when touched.
Did they mistake the road
                    for a stream, boiling away
                    into the cloudy sea?

III.   [If I suffer, let it be in high places]

What, then, is the opposite of human?
Of girl?
                    It swoops,   flies,
          retreats.
                              Swift arc in the air: aerie
                              to archipelago,
                              dream arpeggios.

Once, I strung a wire
from my roof to yours. I walked that steel

thread with no parachute, just an umbrella,
          the wind threw a fit
          and I fell.   Carry me over

          this mountain blindfolded, dear one.
          The altitude hisses in my ears. Carry

me on the palanquin of your body, leave
me on the silent ridge with the ruins
            of a jet crash. Metal wing hangs off its socket.

            The radio signal is broken
and so are my arms.
My hair is burning down
                        but what I see

surprises me: behind dread, a lighthouse;
            behind mourning, a weather vane;
                        behind the trees, a tiny skiff departing.

The White-haired Girl

After the 1945 revolutionary opera of the same name

1945

I will return your spurn with a curtsy
whipped in boiling water.
Cut the red ribbon from my hair,
what's left of my youth. Lotus seeds slide
down your throat—do they taste chaste?
The fugue of winter casts shadows
on the furnace—how it glowers
like the limpets buried in my hair,
handfuls of which you pull
toward shore, toward stagnation.
My destination is not this village,
where boars shear bad skin
in the river, dung and alderflies
thirsting for flesh. Am I maid
or mendicant? The unwrinkled bed
is not what sky aches for. I am no swooning
debt. Next I say *escape* and small gullies
bloom before me—dendriform paradise:
mountain, grotto, kindling. The lightning
in my temple wards off wolves. I bow
only to pick the ticks off my shoes,
brand them clean across your cheekbones.

2011 redux

I stirred five bullets
into your burned porridge,
stole the money you sewed
into the mattress, and took a bus south
of my sorrow—approaching sand,
approaching steel. I couldn't stay
another weekend, peeling roaches
from their graves. Out on the highway
to Half Moon Bay, I saw a power
line detonate a flock of geese.
Another lonely city emerges
from their sooty feathers,
and across the magnetic fields,
taxonomy of aurochs run west
of their extinction. Should I be
embarrassed for trying to survive?
I turn inside-out between
motel sheets, prisoner
of altitude. A child mistakes
a strand of hair for lightning
and the signals of far satellites
question your penance. I won't go
to bed hungry. I wait for your footsteps,
slicing an apple with a borrowed knife.

The Pickpocket

LESSON 1   BEG

In the real story, a girl asks for cloth
because sweat has decomposed her dress.
Ask: *What lie is worth the risk of believing?*
She is easily charmed. Fabrications slip
between her knees. Not all silk is smooth
or sodden mud, but the way she grovels,
knees skinned against gravel, you would've
thought her whole life was spent in pursuit
of clothes. Or tenderness. Hands shove
her down a well. A sewer fills with dark hair.
She combs the water thick with fat loam.
Pulse, extinguished, perfect: she tastes something
red, congealed. Her tongue goes bad for days.

LESSON 2   GIVE

She writes on the cloth: In November I went home with my pickpocket.
Ghouls huddled beside us as he snored. I covered his mouth and stole
back my money but not my sediment. Not my grief. The glutinous
bed: that, too, had an edge. His hands were pendulums that slashed my
hips. As if to say, *This is not what I wanted. This is not what I stole.*

LESSON 3   FORGIVE

The story goes. She climbed back up the well.
Vanished into the jungle for one month, three.
Stomped the nubile grass.

The mountain she stood on was low—it sunk
toward the sea. Rumor has it, she trained
                    her pulse

to stop. Rumor has it, her fingers grew
inches nimbler tying birds with thread.

Her legs elongated as she carried off her animals,
flesh trailing bread and stone.

Stones turned into Andes
and somewhere past Bogotá,
                    a thin stratus tied tight the yarn
                    in the clouds, in her lungs

until they grew taut, until she forgot
                    the city, and salted all her meat
                    with silt and sweat.
Eyes yellowed,
          pricked needle. She stitched

them shut with two threads.
          Map of seven bells. Five pillories.
A hundred pockets.
                    Eight compass points:

She hitchhiked north.
Some girls follow the river.
Some girls follow the scud
of their arrows. Some girls
follow their enemies.
She was one.

LESSON 4 VACATE

She writes on her palm: My lowest point was here, marked by X or Y.
The nadir of the woods, the scurf. I saw the sun split a trunk in half. All
my clothes ruined in heaps beneath me. Was it tornado or vortex that
tore it open? I was naked in the open air, the mange of black thorns
eating me like ants in the red field. The tide thrashed in the distance
as if struggling from its noose. I asked the wilderness to build me back
up, though it was foolish, because who can trust the wilderness? Who
can trust a scenery that remote?

LESSON 5 APPROACH

Good advice: you cannot follow the dead
but you can follow a legend until it stains you
                on the lips, jaw, teeth

until you are its primary evidence.
The school lies just beyond the marauded
graves. Surrounded by yellow trunks,
                    it ages like an inheritance. Covered,
                    covert, the manor's flanked with fallow.

Morning sun shatters the trees. There is no shearling
to wrap their thin forms. The girl is struck
by the synchronicity—a maypole
            of bodies,   a procession—

                    each day the smooth ones rise,
press their swift fists over their even swifter
hearts and murmur,   *Their possessions are airtight*
                                but I'm aerodynamic.

Arcs of fingers cleave the air.
This is the school of seven bells.
A pickpocket's academy. University for thieves.

LESSON 6:   PICK

Pick the lock before the pocket,
so any prison they build for you
will lead you to another corridor,
dank with spillage from imagined
cargo. If it's cold, do not shiver.
If it's hot, do not sweat.

Pick the boy whose backpack

is light. Pick the boy with the sooty
fingers and slippery jacket. When you take
from him, leave the morsels. Leave
the picked-over bones. Pickle the food
you don't eat and store it in a metal
box for your future self to consume.
Because your future will always be hungry.

LESSON 7:   SLASH

Booby-trapped trench coat: first parry the bells,
then fishhooks. Claw until swells jewel the wrists.
Don't go first for the stranger whose purse holds troves.
Don't go first for the territorial eyes.
The lines of the province arrest her.
Infection. Infraction. Sleeves oiled in broth and soil.
In every movie there's a criminal beaten with a shovel.
There are glue traps in the lapels. Finger traps
in the pockets. Make one sound and flunk the test.

LESSON 8:   THANK

She writes in her notebook: Yesterday I held my thumb out by the
side of the dirt road. Any mile further on this circulation, cartilage

would have leaked from my knees. A couple picked me up. In the car, my captors asked me where I was from—Japan? I said Lima, but they insisted *Japan* until I agreed. *I was born in Yokohama, but grew up in Kobe. In 1994, before the earthquake, I left the country on a one-way ticket...* That evening, they offered me a tangle of cash because *you are a woman alone.* I declined, but later as they slept I cut the money out of their bag.

LESSON 9:   TAKE

She pursues the contaminated road
to the richest city, spilling rags along the way.
No stealth. No susurrus.
Having failed the test for pickpockets.
Having dropped out of the thief's academy,
Having stolen every carillon and diamond,
lonely with theft and the coals of invisibility.

LESSON 10:   RUN

Never accept any gifts
because you are a grifter.
Never take a bus. The trick
is to wear a darker plumage,
because umber is armor

against search parties. The trick
is reflex, swift and unarmed—
no weapons except for small knives
you conceal with one finger.
You do not know the contents
of what you're stealing.
The trick is to dash any proof
you are female. Skid
the pavement. Deflect the gaze.
Scan crowds for signs—look
for a particular glance at the sky,
a lope of the eyelid. Trap
your own in a cowl. Hands out,
claws inside. Last week in Tianjin,
a woman in a red down coat
was caught on camera slipping
her hand into another woman's purse.
Lost her incisors, her feral
spine. She was uploaded
for everyone to see. Never wear
red when you're running.

II.

Searching for the Queen Bee

Outlast, outgrow, outshine
all midnight, all opposition.
For sweat & fists don't silence

you, but the gridded landscape
does. Go ahead, run to the garden
where childhood sinks inside

the lake's lips. Wash your face,
its dark adult spot. Believe
in the dawn behind the giant

tree, the light's torn dress,
redress. If you're tired
of fighting, how do you find

the Queen? She's all appetite
and aplomb in runny regalia,
so moist you latch on. Life

is not dear unless coveted
things are claimed: the joy
of exploding queens crackling

in jaws, tougher than goat
and sweet thorns. Honey sticks
to horse manes, rat hide, pigeons

electrocuted on fences,
damp newspapers, headlines
explaining cruelty, cruelty.

Honey drips from glaciers.
May you never sleep, badger:
ever-droning, ever-hunting.

Hurling a Durian

This is the fantasy fruit: it can awaken
desires lodged deep inside a person

> but stuck, like an almond clogging
> the windpipe. The smell of a durian

may erase a child's immediate memories.
So I am addicted, of course. Not to eating

> but to sniffing it like glue, my fingers probing
> its dry, spiked surface until they bleed

and I eat. But the feast disappoints
me because its taste replaces the corpse

> scent with something sweet and eggy,
> a benign tang I flush down with wasabi.

For there is nothing a kid like me
can do except awaken to loss and wish

> for a seven-piece suit of armor. The desire
> always returns: durian as a weapon of truth.

Even if I don't know how to pull a trigger
or whet a knife, it's tempting to imagine

> throwing a dangerous fruit at the head
> of the person who failed you, who hurt you,

who, for all these years, has tried to break
you. But this desire is lodged deep

                    for a reason: the pull of forgiveness
                    like a hopeless gravity, and always, I try

to resist. So I do by taking a spoonful
to my lips, savoring the smear, the din

                    of my cleaver hacking the husk, the juice,
                    the sweat ripping open the rind.

Monstera Deliciosa

I'm a monster because I poison the children.
They dance around me and my fronds flutter
with holes. They invite: *Eat my fanged fruit.*

Each scale will peel off easy, but if you eat it
unripe, it will steal your voice. Your gums
will blister little stars. You'll vomit, swell, tremble.

When ripe, it is sublime. Better than banana,
soft mango, sweeter than wild yellow rambutan
coated in syrup. It only takes one year. Bite.

The Azalea Eaters

Mother begs us not to eat the flowers.
We scrape the pots for blubber. Fat
scalds our dreams, broils our sweat.

    Softly, azaleas kill our hunger.
    Because we believe in pink spadix,
    the fragrance pollinates our tongues.

Before the farmers bulldoze them,
we smuggle fistfuls into our knapsacks.
Now we are sick but only as sick

    as the river that fed us golden tadpoles.
    The river is a gutted diorama: the dire
    wolf, awakening, spits out teeth & fur.

————————◆————————

In our retching, we summon the aphids.
We enter the malnutritive night.
    Stag beetles & horntails

swarm the wax leaves, calm
    the poisons in our too-hot
    cotton mouths.

In our fevers, we summon summer.
    Weevils swim the length of lake. Toads
    tease us with their fat slime.

No water makes us believe we have gills.
Frogs hatch from fuzz. We pity their birth.

———————◆———————

It's the eleventh season of hunger. *Ding dong,*
belts the frog in the muck. *Ding dong,*
sings the salamander.

Fetal and feral, we curl
in our beds.
Fetal and feral, we drink
in the dusk,
hands damp with loam. Old cures
for sadness
don't work anymore—

———————◆———————

ailing, we lean against the window,
mother's ailanthus
& mother, panicked,
wilt on the sill. We grow red welts.
We ask her, *Will we grow red whiskers.*
We ask her, *Will we grow red feathers.*

She covers our mouths,
breathes, *Hush hush.* How will we fall asleep
now that the skink has grown a new tail?

———————◆———————

We've eaten toad, weevil, roe. We'd eat a houseplant
or your pet. We've kissed poison flowers & retched
it all but we're hungry still. In the forest we pantomime

guns with our hands. *Bang, bang*: let's kill the deer, drag
it by its hooves to the fire pit. Gather its juices, grease

the grasses. Hunger strikes—our teeth, our laughter—
we'll eat & eat & eat: it's our rebellion & our disaster.

Capsaicin Eclogue

The Trinidad Scorpion is shaped like a wrinkled
valentine. Its taste exudes mudslide, the hurt
of long fortnights—kettle whiplash, Bunsen flame,
red-blooded bullet. Tongue a piece of tinder.
Driftwood mouth. Brown tongue, yellow tongue,

miscegenation of burnouts. Raw white, yolk drains
through gullet, burning spigot. But the scorpion
doesn't only sting—these seeds cross borders,
travel through sense and tissue, drill into eyeballs,
stampede the remote throat. Have courage: swallow.

Dance in all the forest fires of the future: Tingle—
Tangle—Sweat—Heave—Spin—Break
dance! Mix the pulp. Snakes snap their jaws
through stomach lining. The furniture melts
and outside, the cool evening breaks your legs.

Tag the building with your spit! Each little devil
fits inside your hand: Naga Vipers. Infinity chillies.
Naga Jolokia. Taste one million Scoville units.
This is how tongues make mistakes. Your name
in lights, on stranger lips. Your lips, in red myth.

Mad Honey Soliloquies

4.   [Xenophon, 401 B.C.]

The soldiers straddled thorn hedges
to sneak a taste. Along the Black Sea,
the honeycombs rose like marmalade jars.
Laurel, scorched oleander, and honey,
that yellow voltage. I tried a drop myself.
Some tasted ambrosia.
Some heard prophetic hymns.
Some cringed at tremors blooming again,
youth in their chests, windshorn Eridanus,
then in the sky, an atomized sun.
And me, I got nothing.
Just another lonesome breeze
freezing my ribs until my muscles
stopped moving. Finally I spat it out.
Like that, my men snapped forward,
purging everything. They purged the honey,
the oleanders, the olives. They purged the suppers
of all the nights they'd ever pined.
They purged the junipers, the stars,
the salt and seaweed. They purged the ocean,
the canker, the long fortnights
spent far away—the Zagros mountains
unlike any hillock back home. Imagine:
a whole field of grown men on all fours.
Armored men in full panoply.
Even through all of this, I fell asleep

half-hoping for a vision, insight, anything.
I would have taken intoxication,
even gagging. As I led these young men
through the waning terrain, the only
prayer I dared was *rid us of our collective needs.*
Socrates once asked me: *If all memories*
are theaters, then what can we make
of the shadow scenes, the ones that lurk,
unseen and unexplained? The question came back
when I saw the dew blind them.
And then at dawn they rose like revenants.

5.   [Pompey, 67 B.C.]

It was swarm season—of honey and carnage:
one moment men scavenged, the next they were carrion

under an orange sky. It was swarm season
and before you could count to ten, quivers raked,

stars aimed, a thousand twigs rustled, fell.
Honey and carnage—divesting us of reflex.

It was swarm season. In the sweltering evening, blood
was scented, pure delphinium. Honey and carnage—

Delphi once prophesied: *The man who eats* meli chloron
can speak only truth. Whose sentence was this,

the pleasure of green honey? Ribs flashed,
tongues wagging, sliced off, churning, stumps for speech.

It was swarm season—over before anyone
could bray. But a few mouths cracked open in surprise.

In Lhasa, the sunshine is murdering
everything. Bears faint. Red
goral twitch inside rifle grass.

The white men brought an arsenal
of names. Their skin drips and peels.
Ward and Cranbrook, concerned

for my sallow skin, offer me nostrums
to try, half spit and half bread. Early May
deranges us all—pollen teases from purple

corollas. The honey that locals offer
in shallow bowls is poisonous, but do we care?
We're hungry. Ward acts a drunken fool—

toasting the British émigrés, scattering
popcorn on their tombs. Cranbrook,
not so lucky, staggers into the backwaters

of the Adung. But when I eat the honey,
I levitate. I go seaward—skin flensed
off a whale, coating me in brine. As a boy

in Haita, I once watched dead sharks
wash ashore beside the steep crags.
The stench was enough to empty a gut

of all longing. I sleep three days in the sea
with no end, thinking: *This is how I die.*
With honey and flowers. I die the son of a fish—

trustful servant, too much obeisance.
Snakes bite the petals off their botanist's
specimens. Poor inflorescence—all the tea

in this town tastes feral. Even gold
spins into dung. It lays our dreams
into the bowl where we waste them.

The Spring of Terrible Fevers

oh you who are young, consider how quickly
the body deranges itself…
                    —D.A. Powell

I.

In February, a fortune-teller
ran her fingers over my palms
& said, *dear, you're cursed. let me help you*

fix yourself. When I recoiled,
the season began: a slow,
beating bicycle.

II.

That spring I learned about Ginsberg's
Chinese lover—the one from Shanghai
who panfried their suppers on winter nights.

Later they'd lie on the cot like a pair of hatchets.
The ginger & chives he tossed into the wok,
he tasted on his lover's breath.

III.

In March I caught a horrible disease,
my windpipe catching fire. For twelve nights
I retched into the sink, cast in a spell

of bloodless quivering, this heat-filled dreaming
about somebody's faraway music, prophetic
between   heart/liver/tourniquet.

IV.

That spring I learned about Chairman Mao's
propensity for virgins. He called each girl *mei mei*,
& coated their bodies with plum juice.

Their cries kept his skin ruddy like Buddha's.
To each ear he crooned metaphors of fruit:
      pears/peaches/avocados/apples.

V.

In April, my fingers cold as chess pieces,
I salvaged heat, miserly, hopeful.
Sick boys & girls marched beside me, asking:

When to touch?
Where to navigate? Why this roiling
    inside the blood?

VI.

That spring I learned about flesh, its riverbeds
of silt. I ate spicy gooseberries to still
this oxytocin—the chemical of trust. Next to me,

an androgynous boy played the piano, smiling
with cold olives in his mouth. & I tried
hard to calcify.

VII.

In May, the windows opened, washing
our bodies of thirst. His teeth-scrape, his *shhh*
left me barren, spiritless. I kissed him goodbye

on the stone rotunda, follicles
stinging, skin molting like a lizard's,
    & how I wanted to run.

The Bullies

In 1997, the days were long, the sun
bloodshot, and Mountain View, CA smelled
like duck shit. Those days, everyone's mind

was a sex tape on repeat. Hirsute rumors

clogged the shower drains. When young girls
disrobed together in a locker room, rancor
smelled like petunias. The whole stink glowed

with mutant love. In 1999, tremors erased

my larynx. Voice mails flooded with cackles,
inboxes sneered. Late afternoons, my legs
greened Granny Smith-style, and I believed

when they called me leviathan.

Ovoid girl—black hair, burnt skin, snaggletooth
and sexless ruin. I saw tumors grow the size
of California. Nobody spat. Only suggested.

Give this up. Shucked each desire.

Evenings, when I was finally free, I saw crushed stars
roll into the thistle field. On that pungent summit

I was a gutter, a bountiful gutter. I collected
clean rain. I was a passageway to the open shore.

Lessons on Lessening

In the rigmarole of lucky living, you tire
of the daily lessons: Sewing, Yoga, Captivity.
Push the lesson inside the microwave.
Watch it plump and pop and grow larval

with losses. Watch it shrink like shrikes
when they dodge out of this palatial
doom. On the sky's torn hemline, this horizon,
make a wish on Buddha's foot. How to halve,

but not to have—how to spare someone
of suffering, how to throw away the spare
key saved for a lover that you don't
have, save yourself from the burning turret

with the wind of your own smitten hip.
Do you remember how girlhood was—a bore
born inside you, powerless? How you made
yourself winner by capturing grasshoppers

and skewering them? You washed a family
of newts in the dry husked summer, wetted
them with cotton swabs before the vivisection.
That's playing God: to spare or not to spare.

In the end you chose mercy, and dropped
each live body into the slime-dark moat.
Today is a study in being a loser. The boyfriend
you carved out of lard and left in the refrigerator

overnight between the milk and chicken breasts.
Butcher a bed, sleep in its wet suet for a night.
Joke with a strumpet, save the watermelon
rinds for the maids to fry in their hot saucepans.

Open your blouse and find the ladybugs
sleeping in your navel. Open your novel
to the chapter where the floe cracks and kills
the cygnet. Study hard, refute your slayer.

Song, with Caution Tape

Some kisses make me want to blow up
everything in my satchel—wallet, birth certificate,

checkbooks and all. Headless dolls roll
out. I watch their plastic rib cages melt in starbursts,
               drip like watermelons
onto the crater of my lap.

Through my binoculars, I saw a man blowing air
               into an inflatable woman,
and she grew tall, and taller
               still, until she burst, carbon escaping
until she muttered and wailed, all splayed
               on the floor, glued there until he kissed her.
At this point I stopped watching.

Most days I prowl, a piranha
restless in fresh water. Some kisses make me eat holes
through wet kitchen towels until my teeth shine

               with detergents. Some kisses
turn my tongue green, so even peppermints
               taste like bile. Some kisses are scabs
too bloody to scratch, yet I scratch them.

How can I will the puke not to escape?
               How can I stop it before it takes
leave of me, the way it did when I saw that man
               kiss my mother in the dark

of their laboratory so many years ago?
Some kisses are not without
cruelty. Some things burn more quickly in the ocean.
Even now, as we stroll through the empty
            city at dusk, as you lean in,

and I sand your face between my palms,
my other self is in the mountains
            watching you,
where the distance is safe and the tides are calm.

Suspension Theory

*...maybe love is a mosquito net between the fear of living and
the fear of death.*
                —Francis Bacon

Maybe love is a hammock.
Maybe love is a bone spur.
Maybe love is a science beginning with pomology—

      (sliced open grapefruit, leaking durian, papaya seeds
      scattered like panicking ants)

& ending with anatomy. The esophagus. The bowels.
The small bully in the chest blows a horn.
Inside the sacs of alveoli, little soldiers crawl.

--------◆--------

The mattresses in this city
disappoint: no strangers, no ostriches,
no exploding stars. Even the orioles scatter
at my invitation.

At cocktail parties, I pluck fruits from sangria
& eat them. It is a good way to get drunk
without realizing.

When I met you, we did not speak.

Gravity is dirty, we both agreed.

------------◆------------

Inside the forest of firs & floodlights,

we rifle through the garbage,
starving again. Midnight—marzipan apples.
Rivers catch fire,
sequoias splinter, thumb-slice.

Have our lungs flown with summer tanagers? Children cough
against the galleons. Scales grow from their tiny earlobes.

There are landscapes for this kind of killing.
Against our birthday cakes we are miniature
as the burning candles.

------------◆------------

I am that mosquito.
I am that scourge.

All night, as you loll in cane sugar sleep,
I bite into you, I draw blood.

Itch constellations.
Orion's belt, little dippers

redden your lower back.
Under neck, the poppy fields.

In our small chrysalis we are doing it
to an aria of fluttering insects.

Dear rotten peach:
Dear brown banana:

My job is to awaken you
to that thirst, that drumbeat: skin.

————————◆————————

Matchboxes filled with frozen cider.
Clouds & fisheries. How the smoke champagnes
the sky. Eyebrows waft in wind
like cattails.

> Boat holding mountain, snowcapped void.
> The gingko tree bows down & every cluster
> is a clump of hair.

When we sleep together,
> your head rolls from under me.

————————◆————————

Evacuate the dead house.
The man who lived there lived with mice.
He saw those little bodies flourish
in the winter. They shit little fat rice curds.
All over his sheets, counters, even the green light bulbs.

All over his paintings—when they dried, they dried in mouse shit
& the brown of the shit became the earth.

The brown of the shit became the hide
of the camel.
The brown of the shit became the hoof
of the goat.
The brown of the shit became the cud
of the cow.
The brown of the shit became the smooth
of the skin.

———————◆—————

Who is done with love, raise your hands. Good.

Now, the screaming pope.
Now, the listless bagpipe.
Now, we part in Belleville. You go to Montmartre.
I go to the Seine. I see the dead Jesus. You see a fountain.
Doves dive down from the crests.
You once said that the clouds housed dovecotes.
I do not believe you.

———————◆—————

Evacuate the dead town.
Anthracite burns in bedrock.
Absentia: what does it mean?

> Split urn. Lattice torn from hinge.
> Toilet seat, floorboards, pale wrung clothes.
> Rogue swallet swallowing footprints.

The wind undresses somebody's girlfriend.
A boy gets on his knees. The alcove, an altar:
pecans, persimmons, picture of a woman; she is dead.

Intruder! Don't freeze. Do not step onto the sod.
Where is your hair? Where do you sleep?
How do you know me & why are there tears?

--------------◆--------------

Be lemons.
Be bicycle.
Be the thing that explodes.

Take this map, this math
        of vertigos
& toss until it nets the mountain.

Ask only questions like,
What kind of dessert would you like?

Strawberry or
Orange molasses? Or both?

--------------◆--------------

I, too, don't know what is coming.
Up ahead, the peddlers sell horses

in oblong cages. A woman bites into
a crawdad, inventing semaphores of light.

This rain is anything but baptismal.
It only makes me want to misbelieve.

Above the cliff, a Yunnan temple explodes.
A bedroom bulges with symphonies.

I strap my snowshoes to my boots.
How is it that muscle only gets us this far.

Beyond my body, the suspension bridge
swings to the trills of sudden death.

Honey Badger Palinode

But a broken badger may be a sad
thing after all—the sight of her, all slack-jawed,
sallow: a sneer but no sledgehammer, mouth
      but no meat. In those beads
for eyes there is no obsidian.
Only a gleam, thread stringing thorn & iris
together. It lacks control.
It lacks beauty.   Cells shiver

through the walls that contain them
until they reach the outside. Air fleshes
the daylight.   The badger shakes. Skin
flakes break off, snow from a hanging roof.
Because she is nocturnal, she prays to night
for mutation. It is no   good to want

transformation: lighter feet, aerodynamic
     claws,   keener eyes   to screen
the bodies in the grasses. Panic cannot ford
the river. Sacrament, meat, corpus.
Even the thickest skin is still a membrane.

III.

Migration Suite

the place I'm from is no longer on any map
—Myung Mi Kim

I.   Transatlantic Flight

My tenement is empty. My love is cured. And leave-taking?
What of it? The spadix in this spathe says nothing, says go.

—whips of cirrus? skeleton leaves? disquieting drone?

Please let my marrow go.

—gastropod? taproot? denouement? meditation?

Please let my unburned energy
spill over the coastlines like rain or ruin.

—hurricane? paint box? pandora? floodgate?

Tree after tree, exploding for miles.

Ask the person in the seat beside
where is this place to you?

All your life—

—a sunrise?   fata morgana?   an incubation?
—an airship?   a war howl?   a love confession?
—a fiberglass bed?

SFO—O'Hare—JFK—Schipol—
Malpensa—Narita—Incheon—Tianhe—

Tell me how you feel when you take off.

> *I imagine a star. A clove bullet*
> *ripping through me. Perspiration,*
> *and my love my ghost purring beside me.*
> *A hum. Her sweat tastes like the tea*
> *we drank at the hotel last night.*
> *We're still parked on the tarmac,*
> *but here I am praying*
> *for the error that binds us here.*

II.   Land's Pull

Half-dressed in shudders, the girl could be me
                    but it's my mother.

Tonight she thirsts for bells, gnaws bitter
                    melon, sings "Midnight in Moscow".

Ambrosia: radios crunching throats.
                    Across the red sorghum,

the country eating her alive—
                    boots, neon jacket, red shoestrings and all.

Outside her palanquin,
                    a pulmonary coaxing, singing orbiters.

Hooves can't stir and horses wait. Amaranth
                    and dead earth swarms with foxfire.

The train rumbles by without her,
                    vox nihili. She ducks inside the theaters,

where soldiers dressed as bridegrooms come at her.
                    The gag in her throbs bigger.

She's certain she may be the hostage they're looking for.
                    She's thinking if she'd just surrender.

They'll move her, mar her, marry her
                    across the land of blind sharpshooters

through the airtight sockets of winter.

As long as dawn breaks liquid as lucre and she can catch that last express home.

As long as she can sprint through sorghum taller than any horizon she has known.

III.   Unbearable Nest

All there is in this town: a museum of preternatural history,
where every weekend my love and I yawn at reliquaries.
Behind the glass, dire wolves once uncovered in tar pits snarl,
bereft of thrashing.

                    —Tumulus, tabua, scrimshaw.

What does the night bring? Surely sex lined with fear—
surely the body grinding against silence. Visions of moths,
wasps, and ants cocoon our movements, sucking
us from the air mattress until we are a smitten heap.

                    —Torque, trench, infrared.

In the well that is gagged, I no longer want
for light to carry me. Here I sit strangled by language.
In the hour of the rabbit, I am never awake.

                    —Nacelle, volt, cairn.

Name this. Name this earth. Name this carpet, this gravel,
this shale, this loam. Our apartment evokes the deaths of cygnets.
A party dress, a parting address, the intolerant roots
and our feet bound, our blood, vulcanized.

IV.   Immigration

Howl forever if you must, but it will never be music.
Make deaf monkeys out of everyone.

> *Father you leave us without explaining but I heard*
> *the rumors saying you can heal or fatten the wound*
> *on your knees with the clot of a stranger's country.*

Sepals crown this city of sloughing light.

> *Maroon us here in the flying city.*
> *If your heart is a stuntman fishing for ice then mine*
> *is a cold ingot gilded to the stairs.*

Sorrel, sorrow, spumes of science furl
over your reddening sclera. Your breath
beneath the ochre. What troubles make
you?

> *The kind of father I want is one who will dig a hole*
> *through the floor of his home to find a deeper womb for me.*

Ask the earth what it will feed you.
The truth is a pyrrhic purring—listen
on the airship with crackling ears.

> *Father I thought you were a revolutionary! Every day*
> *you were gone I anticipated my own journey to the West.*
> *I was the Monkey Princess. I sketched a different charcoal*
> *portrait of you every day.*

Here is the lesion on your couch, the tomb,
the television. Take what is abandoned,
thresh the silver from the dross. When the water
crosses the dam, be ready and on your knees.

It is not a life if your neck is (/not) soaped with sweat.

Set your watch back, the rain is beginning.

V.   In Transit

On the train to Milan on an empty stomach.
Two bananas, carrot bisque, spread of fish scales.

> Flummoxed compass—I'm dreaming
> A vessel where the morning limns
> These limbs with sweat.

Outside I find sojourners.
How do they sleep in this awful wind?

> She is wrapped in blankets, but her cheeks
> Still peel off gold as gingko.

A missed missive. This hotel room, this failure of flight,
This dawn where you muffle my waking.

You and I are two parallel rivers
Scudding in opposite directions.

> My blood, the stuntman.
> *Love, let's stay here,* you say to me.
> Another law I shuck
> From this straggled bone.

What if I told you to eat my red corona,
What if I told you to eat my breeze and my bullets,
What if you hang glide over my marled barb—

On the last night of Midnight Bike Ride, I fly over the city's velodrome.
Ovum of my crushed helmet, awaken me from my bike accident!

VI.   Preface to My Unraveling

I ruined my body for a restive life.
To be an exile, a threnody's burning.

The nightmares hammer—wearing a diaper, losing teeth,
everlasting nosebleed, spindrift oozed
                    from molars.

            A caper of erasers chars these passageways.
Junk in the organs, kinks clone the thyroid,
diaphragm punctured like a paper lantern
                            blown out.

                Headed north with wrecked kidneys,
                afraid to see a doctor,
                afraid to empty pockets.

        Roadkill awakens in carbonated rain.

Cirrus glowers with rumors. In the hour
                of the police officer's question,
my hitchhiker mouth is stranded.

Here are my bloodstained sneakers.
            Here is my wing made of wood and wire.
Am I a crying kvetch in an animal's disguise?

            How can I bear it, the flaws I don't know?

VII.   Green Card: Diary of Flight::

In her early years in Boston, she finds herself paused
                in traffic, inhaling the fuel
of her own failing engine. To her doctor

                she describes it as the smell of power,
the motor sound a fluttering,
                a monster one, the Atlas moth specimen
                she found in the museum.

Snow hides all of her features. She lives in a cave.
                Learns the word *peonies*. Then *crocodiles.*
                        Then *jade.* Cold pendant drums her chest.

Plants things—camellias, silver jade plants.
                She imagines rescuing wicker chairs from curbs
                the way she would rescue
                a child from drowning, a cat from the dumpster.

In her arms she carries tomatoes,
                onions, chicken claws tied with string.

Illegitimate dream: obedient daughter.
                When she looks at her daughter, she makes serious
                wishes. *Please hold your head low, know this world
                has limits.*

Illegitimate dream: moving to California.

> Tonight it is written in her diary of flight—
> *toss out the parka and make a beeline*
> *for sunshine.*

Illegitimate dream: permanence.

> She steeps like warm tea in its electric shadow.

VIII. Visa

I have in my hands the permission to return.
Red stamp on my passport, a promise to depart again.

        Taking the exit off the highway, I misplace
        my hands on the bus. Sleeping businessmen

in grey socks slump beside me. The shy, ashen
light of their suits fences me in, a silent border.

        Tonight somnolence is my direction. Every phone
        conversation transplants the hole in my throat.

This unraveling has a dialect. Diction gasps,
phonemes and pheromones. Tether me, claim this

        circadian wilderness. Whatever space was erased—
        plant me there. Continent snapping with swallows.

The trapdoor in my body leads to a room
in a blue house flooding with water.

        Aerodrome of my demented wonder:
        where is my parachute?

IX.   Itinerary: Transfiguration

In 1782, French brothers invented the world's first
hot-air balloons—Montgolfier-style balloons, introducing
to humans the act of moving, elevated, in a capsule of breath.

> Today I shall set a pack of my most ravenous
> wolves free. I shall trample the gates around my lambs.

> *A vacated world flies.*

> Yes, I am strapping myself to a hangar.
> Yes, I will risk the vertical tumble

like Orville on his maiden flight, sweat
slaking his ears, a beautiful orbit—

12 seconds airborne, attempting to control
this human-made thing so hard to trust:

> —muslin, bike chains, spruce
> —wings, aerodynamic drag, resistance

> *What is this atomic diction we invented?*
> *I gamble in a bleak direction.*

We land in the North. I'll spelunk in the most secret
private properties. We'll gambol in the wet grass, roll

in the tarpaulin, watch the vacated world drone over us,
a flock of swifts derailed by hurricanes.

X.   Transpacific Flight

Ladies and gentlemen, drink your passports, kiss your ginger ale—

You're going home or faraway and this is magnificent. Peruse

the duty-free catalog for hammocks or umbrellas.

Our in-flight film, Kurosawa's *Dreams*, is yours to watch for free. Listen

to the radio. Brahms, Vivaldi, Schubert, all eight movements, yours.

Even the sky is yours. Turn off your devices. This motion, too, is yours.

* * *

Passage into gloaming. Our albatross trajectory,
archipelago rising in our stomachs. Mileage. No shores.
From above, the fuselage resembles a spinal chord.

Imagine the engineers studying the wingspans
of albatrosses, skimming over the lonely spumes
in centrifugal fury: tossing oceans, morass

of spindrift. Standing on a jetty, humans take notes:
                                                Wingspan lengths—

Trumpeter swan: 7-8 feet.
Wandering albatross: 11 feet.
White pelican: 10 feet.

This evening we are a study of ambidextrous
movement, a restive moment in the catapult.

Silver contrails web a pennant for our landings.
Ask the person next to you: what is your earliest
memory of flight?

> *How to describe it, a tiny child's revelation?*
> *An unraveling. Vomit in my paper bag.*
> *When I opened the window for the first time*
> *and saw the light vanishing, the skyscrapers shrinking*
> *through the thunder, I pressed my hand*
> *against the cold glass and through this I saw*
> *the fishtail of another flying city.*

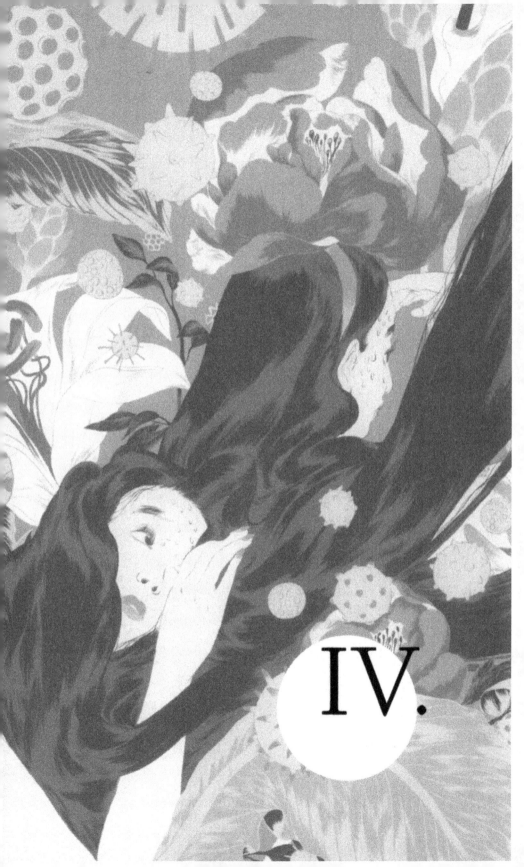

Honey Badger Duet

Our father wanted to kill us
before we were born. Starve us,

stave off hyenas with our youth—
our muscle as protein, lion's bait.

We drained the flummoxed milk
out of our mother, who hissed

at predators. Her sonic cry could shred
raglan to scraps. Now we dance

to shed her from our spines.
The long years tilt—we bite spleen

& anodyne. For all the glory
of gore, we imagine ourselves

dead: asleep inside the culverts,
bald, piebald, very lonely. When

the sky's meat smudges the valley
russet & that blood is so silent

we only listen to snow falling
on distant trains, the hunger stalks

close enough to scoop the pupils
from our eyes & we are danger.

We shovel out old kills from dirt.
Only in sleep do we return

home from hive-coma, disinter
detritus, gulp down the dead.

Yellow Fever

—Gertrude Stein

You are the kind of person who would frame a print of Hokusai's
Dream of the Fisherman's Wife and stroke the airplane
at night, imagining yourself as monster, tentacular
lady-killer. I am the eavesdropper sitting in your ear listening

to everything you whisper—I am smaller than milkweed bug,
and you can't kill me. With the smugness of a man who has
just caught a trout, you say, *I love those Asian women.*
I will fuck you up with the spastic ember of a Puccini opera.

I know what you crave. It is larger than me. It is the pretty
face on the library book—the fallow field, the woman
with a comb in her hair, a grin about her like so many
hives. It is squalid peonies, murderous silk. It is febrile butterflies

and it is slave. It is shedding its clothes and it's shredding your pants
and you are the thing in the plastic bidet. Don't try to musk the malodor—
anyone can smell. You love the feel of socket on tongue? Strip
the pork rind. Shoot the waif. See that smile? Simulacrum.

Tiny waist in jade—you sweat, you slaver. What is this body
to you? Body you subsume—body you misconsume? To have
and to hurt—utter the word *Orient*, I dare you. She may spit
or she may nod. Who's to say the hornbeam awakens to blight.

The Unraveling

Saline satin. Wavelike cusp. Bare shoulder kissed
by leaf, mother of organdy. In autumn, the grenadier
spills grenadine on a girl's pale stomach. Slits the hem
of her corsetry. Breaks its whalebone. The inseam

undoes itself. Lingerie, her appendage for performance,
not pleasure. Paillettes. Latticework. The window designs
titillation. No buttress for nudity, artless hiss.
Somewhere on the road home, she molts, pale

anaconda. Why is red a lurid color? That it evokes
innards? Belt-leash. The stain hangs laundry. O cold
netting made of lace, raveling down thigh on burnt
grass. Somewhere a wish chokes under its strap.

Sartor

After Alexander McQueen

I.

In our slime tryst, you opened
the webbing of my hose,
scattered white flour on my legs.

Under the hood, you cracked
the couture boning
of my gown, and the pangs

II.

that spilled forth made me pass out.
An opulent coma, for I dreamt
of ancient contraptions: whip,

bulwark,   strap-on
glowworm, blackening
your cephalopod lung.

III.

Bioluminescence betrayed us,
my love. To live this hoodwinked
dream, bedeviled knees,

why, I'd give any tank of fuel, truss
or trigger. A bride of plunging
necklines will lose her dolor

IV.

in our indecent space where girls
dress in holograms, X-rays, torn
chiffons. I grow my spine from chic

roadkill. But you, lover, mostly nude,
wear a rust-belt gaze, saliva-
matted fur, pansexual shockwave.

Mad Honey Song

This is my tongue ingesting substance. A picture of a cow, gorging water.

When I eat the honey, I think of your throat above my body, torqued

and throbbing violetly. Your face among azaleas and dung. Whiskey.

Tumbrels carrying dung. Tumbrels carrying lips, endless fingers,

slabs of fresh meat: venison, mutton, goat. Dung describes my lips

on your lips. Dung describes the disgust, the gust, the August mud.

Inland, where my legs stretch into the cold lake, nothing quells me.

You bathe me in a medicinal broth. Too much algae on my lips. Every sip

tastes like slugs. Dawn describes the knives that halve me when you seek

the dung of me. When you're done, I am paper and I am guts, I glut

and seethe. I am your loathing for lentils, your craving for bitter tea.

All the tannins, the metals. The quarries never mined. Quarrels I never

started. Fights I couldn't pick. Forgeries of heat. Never mind.

Homunculus Survival

I.

These days, the hurricanes reeve
through skylines so fast. The roofs collapse
       over our wet heads. Saguaros

      peck at pterodactyl clouds.
We are twins. Students of mutiny. We insist
      on safety, even if we
         contain nothing
            except scales,
    exposed skin, all membranes.

II.

Let's build an aegis
      out of rocks. Let's knit a coat
      out of clouds. Let's planish armor
out of the house that failed
      to protect our ugly frames.

III.

Pariah hour. We eat the food
no one wanted:

beachcomber fodder, skeletal meals
that slowly dissemble, escargot shells
and oxtail marrow. Staccato taste:
the pulps break down.

IV.

Dirty with unguents and easy to bait:
this is how the radio portrays
us. Once, a man asked if he could

touch my hair. *Is it true*
there are magical oils on these strands.

He took me to his house that night.
He wouldn't tell me why; claimed he was sick,
claimed he needed healing.

Wouldn't let me sleep on his bed.
A soggy mesh of genitals
desensitizing the lamplight, quietly.

V.

Live as if kindness is a hoax.
Blame it on our memories. The husks
        of sand creatures moving in streams
where fish curl up, crystallized.

Inside tree trunks, we gambled all our rot
and lost everything. Pity is a cheap emotion,
     and all roads lead to ditches. Hitchhikers
eat cobwebs in darkness,
     resuscitating the roadkill.

VI.

Above the singing sand dunes,
we saw a woman give birth.
Creature made of needles,

clotted flesh, manic seed,
who is the baby squirming
         in vernix?

       Our brother.
The trees in the distance,
yellow trance wounding

the cosmos. Origin of no
returns: orphaned,
water crawls back into the womb.

Lawrenceville Night

Before the bricks,
there were trees, before the trees, there were lovers...
—Terrance`Hayes

This pulse must be quicker
than human—peel back the frog's

single ventricle, yellow petaled
heart pumping brooks & pollen

into the light: O, Bloomfield
Bridge, I can see it through

the chimneys, banners, quiet
chimes. Joyride: tonight

we strap snowshoes to our trunk
searching for the perfect place

to hide from our friends. We find
the house where we broke in

years ago & hacked open a jackfruit,
made our bodies into preserves,

sugared & shrill & terrifyingly ugly.
Lawrenceville's roofs descend

into a bleeding crater, concave lens.
For hours I try to pry my body off

this night, this muscle, stronger
than the axman who hews

off our legs in the groves, our worm-
filled limbs hanging trophies,

bottles & bottles of lungs
where rumors wait, begging to begin.

Haibun for Thawing

I long for an immigrant in my bed. One who is unafraid of knots. One who will arrive with hail on his eyelash. One whose memories are muddy as mine. One who feels the dirt in his marrow. One who guesses the words of his own father's dialects. One whose skin leaps to touch mine. One who follows the floodlights north to me. One who discovers a hideaway, crouching with his palm above his throat where it's warmest. One who trespasses arboretums soaked in manic light. I long to measure his body by its immateriality. Its ability to seep through borders. Someone formed from a womb of passage. Together we will incubate: one sleep, one tic, one uncombed head.

Too far from winter,
The distance to each face grows.
Quiet, said my wish.

Drop-kick Aria

*To lift an autumn hair is no
sign of great strength...*
            —Sun Tzu

Water, arsonist, spring onion, pig—
Show me what it means to be superhuman.

> I will light a match in the basement, flood any attic.
> Teach me how to do. This dojo's already on fire.
> Mentor, I'm a truant for you.

------◆------

When I was a child, helplessness ruled.

Home alone, braving anything, the stain

on the telescope, a bravura of halogen.

> inventory of fear: God, juggernauts,
> giant roaches, mummies,
> stews boiling over, CO,
> bandits snaking up brick—

Unarmed, I wore a nightgown made of paper.

Silt fell from walls. A maelstrom dragged my mama's

dinghy away. Spumes stole the oars, toothed

bangles clamped my ankles. Of course I was curious

about the ingredients of insecticides, the fatal white

powder my father sprinkled against each wall

like sugar. How I tiptoed past it holding my breath

as the roaches died monotonous deaths. Strychnine

adorned their wings. On my mattress, an invisible

dance party. I was always invited, never acknowledged.

Bedbugs writhed across my wrists. An avocado pit

broke my milk teeth. Nerve after nerve, my face was lifted.

————————◆————————

I'm the dunce in my dance class. Can't do a split
if you hold a gun to my head. So I'm shedding that tutu.
Thanks to you, Mentor, I'll do a backflip.

> My place is here, in the dojo. Show me acumen.
> Train me to crack a body with these Glow-chucks.
> Give me plywood. Teach me how to break it down.

————————◆————————

Let's grow braver together, I said to no one.

So I grew up. Nails thickened until I couldn't

tear without wincing.
>   inventory of fear: driving on freeways
>   at night. Infidels. Shucking
>   a mussel. Shadow of muscle.
>   Horoscopes. A man's gaze.

The slime trail followed me onto the street.

In this lightless prefecture, only one dance

hall survived. All evening I stared hypnotized

by the acupuncture chart. Listened to 90's

R&B. My heroines had died. Left Eye, Aaliyah

taught me not to beg for love. *Demand! Pose*

like a boy, wear a hood, they said. I imagined

them as scissor sisters, denuded of flesh,

two beautiful skeletons spinning on the floor.

I wanted to dance with them, feast on genes

and star fruit. If I could do girlhood again, I'd ask

to be scarier. Less whimpering—more pyromaniac

urges, more flirting with kerosene.

----------◆----------

A four-day flash flood, and already there's carrion
in this dojo. Mentor, why too exhausted
        to pick up all the drowned blackbirds?

        With each comes a trail of skinks.
        Don't let me learn your secrets for nothing.
            Fight for them. Charge a price.

----------◆----------

The first time something snapped inside me,

I found a crowbar in the woods. My emotions

stunk of excess, so pure they could only belong

in the gutter. Later, I happened upon a young

spruce—saw myself in its sprigs. Swung once

and missed. Swung twice and needles shook,

left a scar on the bark. How I shuddered

afterward, remembering my only childhood

friend whose name was Shiva, after the destroyer.

That day I adopted her name, picked ticks

out of my hair, punched stone until my knuckles

bled chalk.
> inventory of fear: bones
> breaking. Tenderness
> of skin. Falling off trees.

————————◆————————

In this rooster sunrise, let me believe all fantasies.
Outside our dojo, the sun lifts the landscape, a blindfold
    of gauze. The yew trees have eyes.

> Mentor, don't let me give up, no matter how
> frightened I sound. Teach me ambush, how to mercy
> kill, how to cut with my hands clean.

————————◆————————

If only my father could have seen me then—beating

the shit out of thugs like the son he never had.

It was so easy to deflect their bulk, to dart, shoot,

set traps for their behemoth shapes, boulders

that would crush me if not for my girl's grace.

inventory of fear:
                    Memory. Disturbance.
                    The speed of blood
                    when the skin is cut.
To think that the first time I opened a physiology

textbook, I was met with an image of a cow's red,

pulpy heart. I didn't sleep—my trauma lasted for days,

afraid that such an organ could also beat inside me.

———————◆————————

Today I am struck by how delicate the mountains seem
when, months ago, they looked so indestructible.

Mentor, don't give up on me yet. My superhuman self
emerges from the geyser—ready to tackle, ready to defend.

———————◆————————

One day, the force I was running from cornered

me, caught me in its arms. My ribs broke, my mouth

gorged in. Maybe these bones were cherry twigs

after all! There I was, knife-plunge, coughing red

on hands and knees, everything woozy, as if in

love, the taste of almonds flooding my mouth.

> Skunks found my blood
> in the snow. You followed one,

> found me, took me to the dojo
> where the light danced
> all days and evenings,
> dressing my wounds.

--------------◆--------------

My scooter. My celerity. My roach home.
My beloved dojo. My centrifugal drop-kick.

> If I were more than a string of spit across the eyes.
> If I were more than mote, nail bed, bug.

If only my inventory of fear looked like this:
> Atomic threat. Flying buttress
> collapse. Biological
> warfare. Apocalypse.
> Pretty girl, unsaved.

On the street with whale-lights and trembling marimbas,
> watch me break it down.

Inviolacy

Tonight, we shrink
      for no one. Tonight, we are afraid
            of nothing. Not torpedoes, not the long

bodies of submarines or tiger sharks
      that circle beneath us. Not wilt, not tornados,
            not the dark camps moored to erasure.

We will reel them in, shear their teeth.
      Their husks stew the sea. Tonight, awaken me
            from this dream of apple blossoms. We'll follow

the kingfisher downstream, forget what we're
      confronting. It's better this way. To mythologize:
            city of endless crayon, endless sod;

boy riding bicycle toward Lijiang.
      Chimeras cannot hurt us
            even if they were once matter, pestle

grinding mortar. Even the abattoir
      feels unreal—it's unlikely that we'll ever
            witness: creature turning

into meat. The duck hangs whole
      in the restaurant window. We believe
            it is whole. When we order it plump,

it is cut to pieces in the back room.
Even invincible, we envy the luxury:
a room to bleed in and break apart.

Notes

"Mad Honey Soliloquies 1-3:"

This poem is primarily based on the medical article "Mad-Honey Sexual Activity and Acute Inferior Myocardial Infarctions in a Married Couple" by Mikail Yarlioglues, MD, et al. (*Texas Heart Institute Journal*, 2011). It explains the case of a couple who checked in to a Turkish hospital complaining of heart pain. Over one week they had intentionally consumed honey from the Black Sea region of Turkey in order to "improve sexual performance." They were experiencing "atrioventricular block," among other symptoms, and "impaired consciousness" and were subsequently treated (heart rate returning to normal) and released after five days in the hospital.

"The Azalea Eaters:"

This poem is based on an article headline "Children in Daehongdan die from eating azaleas," (*North Korea Today* No. 154, June 2008). Quoted: "In Sambong Middle School, 9 students were dead from azalea poisoning. Adults know what to eat and what not, but young children çan't tell and just put anything in their mouths because they are hungry."

"Mad Honey Soliloquies 4-6:"

The first section refers to Xenophon, Greek scholar and commander of 10,000 Greek soldiers. He led his soldiers to Trebizond, where poisonous honeycombs grew wild and he witnessed the effects of mad honey. In his collected writings, *The Anabasis*, he describes it:

"but the swarms of bees in the neighborhood were
numerous, and the soldiers who ate of the honey all
went off their heads, and suffered from vomiting and
diarrhea, and not one of them could stand up, but
those who had eaten a little were like people
exceedingly drunk, while those who had eaten a great
deal seemed like crazy, or even, in some cases, dying men..."

—*The Anabasis* (4.8 18-21), translated
by Carleton L. Brownson

The second section refers to Pompey, who centuries after Xenophon led his soldiers through Trebizond where the enemy laid traps of mad rhododendron honey. The soldiers, sick and drunk with honey, were annihilated by the army of Mithridates, the king of Pontus. This information was gleaned from *Honeybee: Lessons from an Accidental Beekeeper* by C. Marina Marchese (Black Dog & Leventhal Publishers, 2011).

The third section is narrated by a minor character, Mano, in British botanist/explorer Frank Kingdon-Ward's book, *Plant Hunter's Paradise*. He was a servant to Ward and his comrade, Cranbrook, through their travels in Tibet and Burma. They studied rhododendrons and thus were susceptible to poisonous honey. F. Kingdon-Ward. *Plant Hunter's Paradise*. (New York: The MacMillan Company, 1938).

"Migration Suite:"

The second section, Land's Pull, is inspired by Zhang Yimou's film, *Red Sorghum*.

"The White-haired Girl:"

The poem is after the contemporary Chinese folk myth, which was adapted to a 1945 opera (and later, ballet, play, and film) depicting a peasant girl, Xi'er, who escapes her captors to the mountains where her hair turns white and she becomes immortal.

Recent Titles from Alice James Books

Split by Cathy Linh Che

Money Money Money | Water Water Water, Jane Mead

Orphan, Jan Heller Levi

Hum, Jamaal May

Viral, Suzanne Parker

We Come Elemental, Tamiko Beyer

Obscenely Yours, Angelo Nikolopoulos

Mezzanines, Matthew Olzmann

Lit from Inside: 40 Years of Poetry from Alice James Books,
Edited by Anne Marie Macari and Carey Salerno

Black Crow Dress, Roxane Beth Johnson

Dark Elderberry Branch: Poems of Marina Tsvetaeva,
A Reading by Ilya Kaminsky and Jean Valentine

Tantivy, Donald Revell

Murder Ballad, Jane Springer

Sudden Dog, Matthew Pennock

Western Practice, Stephen Motika

me and Nina, Monica A. Hand

Hagar Before the Occupation | Hagar After the Occupation,
Amal al-Jubouri

Pier, Janine Oshiro

Heart First into the Forest, Stacy Gnall

This Strange Land, Shara McCallum

lie down too, Lesle Lewis

Panic, Laura McCullough

Milk Dress, Nicole Cooley

Parable of Hide and Seek, Chad Sweeney

Shahid Reads His Own Palm, Reginald Dwayne Betts

How to Catch a Falling Knife, Daniel Johnson

Alice James Books has been publishing poetry since 1973 and remains one of the few presses in the country that is run collectively. The cooperative selects manuscripts for publication primarily through regional and national annual competitions. Authors who win a Kinereth Gensler Award become active members of the cooperative board and participate in the editorial decisions of the press. The press, which historically has placed an emphasis on publishing women poets, was named for Alice James, sister of William and Henry, whose fine journal and gift for writing went unrecognized during her lifetime.

Designed by Pamela A. Consolazio
LITTLE FROG DESIGNS

Printed in the USA
CPSIA information can be obtained
at www.ICGtesting.com
LVHW041925041023
760138LV00002B/232